Find, Meet, and Marry the

Person of Your Dreams

By

Gerald A. Dean

ISBN-13: 978-0692370971
ISBN-10: 0692370978

Published by Dean Corp. Publications

Gerald Dean

P.O. Box 6063

Douglasville, Ga, 30135

You can reach Gerald Dean at:

Email-Geraldadean@gmail.com

Twitter-@Mr_Dean31

IG-mr_dean31

Facebook-/Gerald A. Dean

Closer2Christ.wordpress.com

Youtube-Gerald Dean Live

It is 2am and she is just getting home. Smells like she has just taken a shower, but claims that she is about to take another before she joins me for bed. Late night calls from blocked numbers, frequently catching her in lies, I know that she is cheating and I do not care. In a sense I am glad that she is cheating. Can one of us finally find happiness because joy no longer dwells in this Godless marriage? But what father stops his adult son from making a conscious decision? So the blame is now mine alone to bear. I have not loved her for years but I faithfully carried out my sentence. Thank you for cheating because now according to scripture, I can finally divorce you and have another chance to get it right. Lord please help me to find the spouse of my dreams so that I never have to go through this again.

Sincerely,

Regret

Decide the Type of Spouse You Desire

The bible teaches us in *(Proverbs 10:24, NKJV)* that" the desire of the righteous will be granted!" According to the word of God, we as believers are entitled to and promised by God that we can have the type of mate we desire. When deciding what type of spouse you desire it is important to be able to have a visual picture so when God sends it across your path you can recognize it. After we pray and ask God to help us to find a mate, the enemy whose job is to STEAL, KILL, and DESTROY tries to do just that your prayer. Do not let the enemy steal precious time from your life with a counterfeit mate, kill the promise of God for your life by causing you to be double minded, and destroy the ministry that God has planned for you and your mate. It really hurts my heart when I hear of a person that "was believing" God for a spouse and was deceived and fell for a counterfeit instead of what God had for them.

I believe that after waiting and praying for months and even years in some cases, we want to believe so bad that the prayer has been answered that we ignore clear signs that we are dealing with a counterfeit mate. When I was dating I would always make the mistake of giving a person qualities that they only claimed to have but never showed. How many times have you dated someone that claimed to attend church regularly upon meeting them, and after four months of dating they have yet to attend church? Or that man who said he was a good father but has not spent time with his kids in six months! I believe that the key to avoiding a counterfeit mate is to pay attention to their actions and not their words. The bible teaches us in *(Matthew 7:16, NKJV)* that we will know a tree by its fruit.

Becoming Double Minded

While we are waiting for a prayer to be manifested, our actions should show God what we are believing him to do in our lives. In my book "How to Pray…And Get Prayers Answered!" I gave an in-depth look at how the enemy can hinder or rob us of prayers being manifested in our lives by causing us to waiver. The prayer is then never answered because we are stuck playing tug-of-war with the manifestation of our prayer being answered. Our mouth is telling God that we want a spouse but our actions are telling him something completely different. God looks at a person's actions because it shows evidence of their faith.

If we look through the New Testament we will see that Jesus always responded to faith.   What made Jesus quickly answer prayers was when he looked at the person's actions and saw their faith. The woman with the issue of blood believed that if she could only touch the clothes of Jesus she would be made whole.   The woman then put action behind her belief, fought through the crowd and touched Jesus clothes.   In *Mark 5:34* Jesus said to her, "Daughter, your faith has healed you. Go in peace and be freed from your sufferings."

How God responds to our prayers is directly connected to what we exhibit in our actions.   I had a friend that said he was believing God for a wife, but since "God was taking too long" began to date and sleep around with different women who was not even the type of woman he wish to marry.

His actions were telling God that even if he really does desire a wife, he does not desire to have one right now. Right now he desires to sleep around and "sow his royal oats". There are people in this same situation that has asked God to help them find a mate years ago and that prayer is sitting on a shelf in heaven waiting for them to put some actions behind their words. The bible says in *(Proverbs 18:22, NKJV)* that "He who finds a wife finds a good thing, and obtains favor from the lord."

The key word is FIND, meaning that you have to go and look for her. A man's job is to look for a wife while the woman's job is to allow herself to be found. Faith is always shown in actions so if you are hooking up with or dating people that do not have the qualities you are looking for in a mate, you are double minded. The bible tells us in *(James 1:7-8NKJV)* that a double minded man is unstable in all his ways and will receive nothing from the lord. If you claim to be looking for a mate but go to spots that people generally go to hookup for the night, what are you really looking for? To some it may seem like no big deal but if you think about it, our decisions change our path and ultimately who we cross paths with. Your mouth can lie, but your actions will always tell God what you truly desire.

For this reason it is important to decide what type of spouse you desire. The bible tells us in (Habakkuk 2:2) to "Write the vision and make it plain." When we first decide what type of spouse we desire and make the vision clear, we avoid the chance of becoming double minded or falling for a counterfeit mate. The clear vision keeps us anchored to the promise of God that we can have whatever we have the faith to believe him for. When a potential spouse crosses our path, the clear vision will let us know rather to entertain this new person or not to even bother wasting our time.

An example would be if a woman was six foot tall and was believing God for a tall husband that is at least six foot three. The woman has decided that a man's height is high on her "must have" list and now has a clear vision of how tall the man of her dreams will be. Now when this woman is out and approached, she need not waste time dating "shorter" men because this is not the true desire of her heart. There are some that would argue that this concept is a tad bit "shallow" while others receive scripture as truth when God said that the righteous shall have the desires of their heart.

Counterfeit Love

What we want to avoid is counterfeit love. Think like counterfeit money...it looks and feels like the real thing but when you look beyond the surface and put it under the light or take a counterfeit pen to it, you see that it is not real and that it is not what you think it is. You were just looking at the surface of it and what you thought was real and your soul mate is just a counterfeit of the real thing! People spend so much of their life with their counterfeit soul mates because they are only looking at the surface i.e. the nice car, the shoes, the house and all of the things that can change at the drop of a hat and not below the surface. They say they love this person but love someone they only know the surface of and thus have a counterfeit love. It is not a real true love! It is a strong lust. Everyone has those moments in life where they experience a counterfeit love and in the end they may not end up with their soul mate but they have learned something about themselves and what they are really looking for in a soul mate and learning to look past the superficial things of life and below the surface to find the true soul of their partner and eventually their soul mate or the person of their dreams.

Prayer For the Spouse of Your Dreams

Oh Heavenly father in the name of Jesus, I desire a mate. Your word says that it is not good for man to be alone so I know that my desire is in your will. Lord God your word also says that the righteous shall have the desires of their heart and I was made righteous through Jesus Christ. Heavenly father you are not a man that can lie so I believe without doubt that your word is true, and you will stand on your word to completion. Oh Heavenly father I ask that you cause me to be extremely sensitive to the Holy Spirit so that I can easily discern what is from you and what is a counterfeit. I ask you lord God to order my steps and guide my path and help me to find, meet, and marry the spouse of my dreams. I decree and declare that I will find, meet and marry the spouse of my dreams and will not be deceived or distracted by counterfeit mates. Oh Heavenly father I do believe that this prayer was answered the minute it was spoken so I eagerly await its manifestation in Jesus name, Amen.

Discover God's Plan For Your life

A lot of people want the blessings of God but do not want to follow God's preferred path for their life. The key to this thought process is found in *(Jeremiah 1:5, NKJV)* before we were born God knew us. God knew what our strengths and flaws would be. God also knew what our dreams and desires would be. So when God was creating each of us, I believe that these things were taken into account as he created the plan for our life.

(Matthew 7:9-11, NKJV) states "Or what man is there among you who, if his son asks for bread, will give him a stone? Or if he asks for a fish, will he give him a serpent? If you then, being evil, know how to give good

[16]

gifts to your children, how much more will your father who is in heaven give good things to those who ask Him!" Think of it as sort of an arranged marriage. Before you were born your father that knows everything about you created a path for your life. On that path he created divine encounters with people that you would meet and have the opportunity to exercise your free will to date and possibly marry. I believe that a lot of people miss out on a good spouse that God would have preferred for their life because they choose to follow their own path and in doing so rejected what God had for them in the process!

In our human arrogance we somehow believe that we can pick and choose what we want from God and what we do not want. We mistakenly think that we can redirect God's path for our lives and twist it up to our satisfaction. Some years ago, a lady shared a testimony in church that really showed how a person can miss out on certain blessings by not being on the path God wants us on. The lady's testimony was that she had decided to take the day off from work. She was in the kitchen about to cook breakfast and something told her to instead of cooking, go to her favorite restaurant for breakfast.

The lady said that she really did not feel like leaving the house but as she started pulling food from the refrigerator to cook, she continued to feel as though she was being pulled towards the restaurant. After playing tug-of-war with herself, the lady finally gave in and went to her favorite restaurant where she met her husband as she stood in line waiting on her breakfast. The lady never shared with the church just exactly how long she had" been believing" God for a husband, but I cannot help but to wonder if she had not gone to the restaurant that day, would she have ever met her husband? Sometimes God has us to do something we do not feel like doing to get something that we want. For this reason it is important to always be open and in communion with God.

If we are not certain on what to do in a situation sometimes it is smart to do nothing until we clearly know what direction God would like for us to take. Some years back I was dating a woman and prayed asking God if this was the woman he had for me? I wanted to clearly hear what God had to say about this situation so I began a three day fast. On the second day of this fast I went to bed and had a dream that this woman and I were married and I was completely miserable. I saw every one of her bad qualities that I had been over looking for years but this time it was different. In the dream I was able to see and feel how each one of these bad qualities would affect my life if I chose to marry this woman. When I awoke from the dream I heard a voice clearly ask me "Is this what you want?" I soon after ended the relationship with this woman because God showed me how miserable my life would be if I decided to stay with her.

Beware of the Counterfeit

Once you think you have met the person God suggests, make sure it is not a counterfeit. From my experience, sometimes when we are seeking God for something special, the enemy has a way of sending a counterfeit or distraction to attempt to rob us of what God has in store for us. For this reason it is important to have a clear picture of what type of person that you are believing God for. Since no one is perfect there will obviously be "little" things that you will have to compromise on, but if this is truly a suggested mate sent from God, their good qualities should far exceed a few bad ones.

It may seem a bit trivial to make a list but how else will you know when you have met "the one" if there are no guidelines? A friend of mine who we will refer to as Jacob some years back was believing God to help him find a wife when a female friend of his introduced him to one of her girlfriends that we will refer to as Lauren. Jacob and Lauren met for dinner and there was an instant chemistry! There was a strong attraction between the two, the conversation flowed smoothly, and it seemed as though their dreams and goals in life were perfectly aligned.

For the first few months everything was perfect but soon after Lauren began to change. Jacob had a son and daughter from a previous relationship that he was open about with Lauren in the beginning. Lauren said that she loved kids and she would treat them as her own. As the relationship progressed, Jacob would always notice that Lauren made no attempt at developing a relationship with his children. Whenever they would go out she would ask for him to find a sitter and would always avoid interactions with his children. Whenever the children were around everything they did would seem to annoy Lauren to the point that she would leave and go home. After almost two years of dating, Lauren finally admitted that she hated kids. She told Jacob that when they met he seemed like a really nice guys so she tried to "put up with his kids" hoping that one day she could grow to love and accept them. She then asked Jacob to just give her time because she was sure that she could grow to at least like them and be cordial. After the conversation with Lauren, Jacob was completely heartbroken but at least left with clarity. Lauren was a counterfeit! Lauren appeared to be what he was believing God for; possessing almost every quality he wanted in a wife except for the most important thing to him. It was important to Jacob that any woman that came into his life would love his children as their own and he did not have this with Lauren. A dead giveaway that Lauren was not the one was when she admitted to "hating kids" and having to make an extra effort to even be cordial to his children. Remember that when you meet the one sent by God they will be perfect. Perfect not in the sense of having no flaw, but perfect meaning they will be a perfect fit for you.

Be the Type of Person the Spouse of Your Dreams Would Date

I was always raised with the mindset that if I possessed a certain quality I had the right to require that quality in a partner. If I was a kind and giving person, I would not be asking too much for the person I was dating to also be kind and giving. While some believe that if a woman makes six figures a year it is no need for her to require that her partner earn the same, I tend to disagree. I believe that everyone has certain preferences when it comes to choosing a mate and this is their God given right. Since marriage is a lifelong commitment, no one should ever feel that they must "settle" for less than their hearts desire for the sake of being in a relationship. I believe that every good desire comes from the lord and it is hard to believe that God would give you a desire for something that he would never let you have.

The question we are now forced to ask ourselves is, Are we ready to receive what we are believing God for? When you go out in public do you present yourself as someone another person would be proud to wear on their arm? I hear guys all the time praying to God for a super model and leave the house looking sloppy: pants three sizes too big, unshaved and have not had a fresh hair cut in weeks. My response is always "You are not believing God for a wife, you are believing God for a miracle," because it would take a miracle for a woman to stop and talk to you. Just because we include God into a situation does not remove reality and personal responsibility from the equation. The reality is that our appearance matters when meeting a potential mate and we should present our self in a respectable way that attracts the opposite sex. When meeting someone new the two tests you must pass is the physical attraction test and the personal attributes test. The goal is to be the best you that you can be and this in turn will attract the type of person you are looking for. What is your dream career? What is your dream physique? What would you like to accomplish in life? By accomplishing these goals, you become the best "you" that you can possibly be and the right person will be proud to have you on their arm.

Learn to be Social

A lot of times you can know everything you need to know about a person by having a conversation with them. People will literally tell you their strengths and flaws if you will just listen. When I was single I made the decision to simply try and have a conversation with every single woman in Atlanta. I figured that since there are thousands of single women in Atlanta, by the time I have had a conversation with everyone of them, I would have found the woman I was looking for. To the women it would appear that I was just a friendly guy making conversation, when in fact I was stepping out in faith believing that God would allow me to meet the type of woman I was believing him for.

The scripture teaches us that we will know a tree by the fruit that it bears so the conversation would help me to do just that. I believed that one stranger would have no reason to lie to another and by the end of the conversation I would know if the person I was talking to was a potential mate. How can we honestly say that we are believing God to help us find a mate but yet we place no effort in searching or allowing ourselves to be found? Scripture tells us in (Proverbs 18:22, NKJV) "He who finds a wife finds a good thing, and obtains favor from the lord." As men we must find the woman and the woman must allow herself to be found.

Start Getting Prepared

Although being single can be lonely at times, there are positive ways to make the time go by instead of dwelling on what you do not have. Truth is, there is a process with God and a lot of the time we are not ready for what we pray for and must be prepared. Because God will never put on us more than we can handle good or bad, there is always a preparation stage. A stage in our life where God prepares us for the blessings that we are about to receive. There was this woman that found out early in life that there was a problem in her uterus and as a result she would probably never be able to carry a child to term.

The lady began to pray and ask God to send her a husband and because of her medical condition, she told God that she desired a man that already had kids. After the prayer the woman realized that she was not currently prepared to be a mother so she began to prepare herself, putting action behind her words and exercising her faith. The lady began to purchase cook books so that she could cook delicious meals for her family, learned how to do little girls hair incase the man she met had daughters, and amongst other things she purchased a gym membership for her physical appearance. Anyone that did not know this lady would probably assume that she was already married with a family because her actions clearly showed what she was believing God for. Although it took a year and a half, the woman ended up meeting a widowed father of twin girls whose mother died of childbirth complications a few years prior.

Forgive and Let Go

If you have not yet found love could it possibly be because of unforgiveness in your life? Ask yourself the question "Who have I not yet forgiven? This unforgiveness is hindering you from finding the person of your dreams. How can one expect to open new chapters in life while still being haunted by the old? Nothing is more unattractive and will drive a person away quicker than punishing them for something they did not do.

Before finally divorcing my parents were married for twenty-one years. My childhood was spent watching my mother pay the price for the women that hurt my father before they even met. My mother's days were spent caring for her eight kids and never away from us for longer than five minutes. My father however would always accuse her of having an affair and then treat her as if she did in fact cheat on him. My father would say "Every woman I have ever been with has cheated on me and you are going to do it also, it is just a matter of time."

This lasted my entire childhood, any new piece of clothing my mother received my father would reply "You must have gotten that from your other man huh." If my mother wanted to go to the store my father would tell one of the kids "Go and ride with your mama to the store, keep an eye on her." My mother was what many men would consider the perfect wife but my father robbed himself of love and happiness because of his inability to forgive the women in his past and live in the present. Yes someone hurt us in the past, but at this point it is nothing we can do about it. If you were in a relationship for six years with a person and they mistreated you, completely ripped your heart out, please realize that they have already wasted six years of your life and they cannot have another minute of it!

Say: *You hurt me, but I forgive you. You do not owe me anything nor do I need closure. Today I decide to forgive, forget, and put this hurt behind me. I know that what God has in store for my future is greater than anything I am leaving behind!* By taking action stepping out in faith and closing doors to your past, you are showing God that you are indeed ready to receive what he has in store for you. Letting go of unforgiveness has a domino effect because it changes the type of people we attract into our lives. The old

[35]

saying "opposites attract" was referring to hobbies and characteristics, not attitudes.

A person that is bitter and angry at the world because they are filled with past anger and hurt will never attract a loving happy person into their life. Have you ever been with a group of friends laughing, joking around having a good time and someone comes into the room in a bad mood? Do you notice how the joy in the atmosphere is instantly sucked away and you find yourselves trying to get away from this person as soon as possible. This is the same way in relationships. No happy and loving person wants to be with a person that sucks the joy from their life. A bitter and unhappy person will attract another bitter and unhappy person because misery loves company. On the same notion a happy and whole person will be attracted to that of similar nature so decide which of the two you wish to attract.

The Waiting Process

I know it can be hard at times, watching other couples together secretly asking God "When will it be my turn?" Just know that the loneliness you feel now is nothing compared to the joy you will feel when your answered prayer is manifested. Whenever you get lonely or begin to get frustrated, remember the vision. Close your eyes and imagine how it will look and feel when you do meet the person of your dreams. Remember that your prayer for a mate was in God's will and he answered your prayer the minute you prayed.

Remember that God is moved by faith and he loves to watch his children stand on his word and put action to it. The word tells us in (I Timothy 5:13, NKJV) that an idle mind is the devils workshop, so for this reason it is important not to sit around thinking of what you do not have. Use your free time to exercise your faith and prepare for what you are believing God for. If you are a woman believing God for a man that is well cultured, you can spend your free time exploring new cultures yourself so that when you do meet him, there is even more to talk about. If you desire a woman that keeps up with her appearance, you can spend your free time hitting the gym and working on your own appearance.

Do not let yourself become discouraged if it takes awhile to meet the person you are searching for. The media and society has deceived us into thinking of God as a genie that snaps his fingers and prayers are instantly answered, but this is not so. If we look back through the bible everything God did took time. God promised Abraham a son which took twenty-five years to be manifested. David was anointed King of Israel but did not take the throne until many years later. Ruth did meet her Boaz but this union also did not happen overnight.

The bible tells us that a day is as a thousand years to the lord. So what does this mean to us as humans? This means that when dealing with God our whole concept of time is thrown out of the window. For the hopeless romantics this means that you will be minding your own business one day as you stumble upon the person of your dreams. The person that reminds us that fairy tales do come true and life with God can be that of a fairy tale at times.

Rejoice in the Husband or Wife of Your Youth!

The bible tells us in *Proverbs 18:22* that he who findth a wife, findith a good thing and obtains favor from the lord (For Men). And *Proverbs 31* refers to the woman as virtuous and rare (For Woman). In both passages of scripture the bible refers to the mate as being a blessing and a rare find. Because of this we should always treat our mate as a precious gift from God. The love between a husband and a wife should always reflect the way that Christ loves the church. If a person ever wanted to know just how much God really loves them, they should be able to look at the marriage between a husband and a wife and get a perfect visual.

It has been a long journey, you have kissed a couple frogs, avoided counterfeits, and now it is time to rest right? Wrong, anything that is worth having is worth maintaining. The enemy's initial plan may have been to prevent you from meeting the spouse that God wanted you to meet but even though he has lost that battle, his purpose will always be to steal, kill, and to destroy. If the enemy cannot steal the gift of an amazing spouse from your life, he can still kill your joy and happiness by destroying your relationship. For this reason we must always keep God at the center of our relationship and do our part in maintaining the relationship and not giving the enemy lanes to work in due to our own negligence.

Make the Honeymoon Last a Lifetime

When most people think about a happy relationship I believe that they envision the "honeymoon stage" of the relationship where romance is still present and intimacy has not yet left the relationship. It is so depressing to me when someone sees a couple in-love and comments "give them another year or so and that honeymoon crap will be over". In our society who put a timer on how long two people can remain in the blissful love stage in their relationship where the only thing on their mind is each other? How many times have a person stepped out of their marriage and relationship in the "honeymoon stage" when things were still good? This section of the book is an attempt to help couples remain in the "honeymoon stage" of their relationship for the rest of their life. No more side chicks, affairs, physical outlets, or any other name for cheating you would like to use. Now I do understand that some people enjoy variety and will cheat rather everything is phenomenal at home or not...this book was probably NOT for you. This book was intended for the hopeless romantic that dares to be different and bold enough to believe that you can marry the spouse of your dreams and be in love for a lifetime.

Honesty First

In the beginning you are negotiating how you will be treated for the remainder of the relationship. I believe that this is the most important time in the relationship where honestly is key because two people are attempting to see if they are compatible. I believe that a lot of future problems can be avoided if two people just realize in the beginning that they are not compatible. We must realize that everyone has a free will. Everyone has their own "list" of qualities that they want in a significant other. When you meet a person you either will or will not meet their list of criteria and attempting to force yourself onto their list will only bring you heartache in the future. I believe that some of us set ourselves up for failure by tricking the other person into thinking that we fit their criteria when we really do not, like men lying on their financial stability or women saying that they enjoy cooking when they secretly hate it. Always be true to yourself and true to the other person keeping in mind that with God nothing is a "forced fit". All gifts from God are perfect, not perfect in a sense that it is not flawed but perfect being that it is a perfect fit for you.

Boundaries

I believe that it is human nature to test your boundaries. When a child is left with a new sitter for the first time and the parents leave, a lot of times you will find that the child immediately attempts to see what they can get away with. I believe that we as adults never really grow out of this phase because when making a decision to date a person we must be able to paint a visual picture of what our life will be like with this person. I have had friends that would start dating a girl and the girl wants to come across as the "cool girlfriend" so she tells the guy that she does not care if he goes to strip clubs. We then fast forward months later and they are arguing about the guy going to strip clubs. In the beginning of a relationship I believe it is important to identify what you are ok with and what you are not, and be consistent. It is a lot easier to leave a relationship of two months than two years if you see that someone will not give you the respect you deserve or is not able to provide something else that you need from the relationship.

Show Affection

I believe that one misconception that many people have is that everyone displays their love in the same way. I remember growing up my father would never hug or kiss any of his children. This at times was confusing as a child because it made me question rather my father really loved me. I would watch television and see fathers showing their kids a lot of affection and think that this was the norm. It was not until I was in my early twenties that I realized that different people show their love in different ways. My father since his father did not do this for him, showed his loved to his kids by making sure they were always protected and provided for.

I have met women that were not affectionate and thought they were showing their love and affection by having sex. The problem we run into with dating and marriage is discovering how does our partner display love? What is their concept of love? As a child, life has taught our partner how to love, and we may or may not agree with the lessons that were taught. In the beginning of a relationship it is important to talk to your partner about affection and what they think is normal, how much is too much and how much is not enough. During this conversation be mindful that your partner will probably feel extremely vulnerable letting you know how much affection they need. If a male partner expresses that he desires more affection than you think is normal, try not to make him feel feminine for this desire because it will not remove the need, it will only make him pull away from you hiding the void or seek elsewhere.

If the male or female partner is "cold" meaning not really receptive to affection be careful not to make them feel like they are not human because they lack affection. This can also make a partner pull away from you feeling as though you do not understand them, or that you think they are not normal. A good way to determine the best way to show your partner affection is to pay attention to the way they show you affection. A person that enjoys kissing and holding hands probably desires for their partner to show their affection by initiating a kiss or hand holding sometimes.

Sometimes "NO" Kills Intimacy

The world is you and your partner's playground! Every date that you guys go on should be an exploration, something new and exciting that the two of you can check off the list of things done together. When one partner is attempting to be spontaneous nothing kills the mood quicker than "NO". There will be times in a relationship that we have to take one for the team. We may not feel like doing something but if it is important to our partner it should be important to us.

The Game Factor must be thrown out the Window

You must decide first rather you want to play games or be in a relationship. There are silly things that we as singles have been conditioned to do in relationships that are counterintuitive if we ever wish to build intimacy in a relationship. We have all been taught to think like the opposite sex. Don't catch feelings until the other person catches feelings. Don't be the first to call. Try not to show how much you are into them until they make themselves vulnerable first.

Think about the reason why we play games in relationships. We are either afraid that this person will take advantage of our feelings and hurt us or we have control issues and are fighting for control in the relationship.

Either way, fear or control has no place in an intimate relationship. You must first decide rather or not you will trust this person and give them a fair shot at possessing your heart.

A Lifetime of Courtship

Because we as humans are constantly growing and changing, it is important to date our mate for the rest of our lives. Dating keeps us in touch with the person we are spending our lives with and helps us not to grow apart from them. I recommend you and your mate have a weekly date night. One night of the week where you and your partner go out and spend time together.

Some of the Rules for Date Night Is:

- *No talking about anything serious-* Any issues or discussions that need to take place can happen after date night! Date night is the foundation to keeping the flame burning in the relationship and should be treated as a priority.

- ***No talking about the kids or in-laws, unless it is about something funny that happened-***The purpose of having date night is for you and your partner to get away from the stress of dealing with kids and in-laws so it is counter intuitive to bring them up on date night. The key is to keep date night fun with no negativity.

- ***If you are mad at you your partner about anything, you must forgive them before date night!*** - This will force the couple to deal with issues as they happen and not let them bleed over into the following week. And as an added bonus, the make-up sex at the end at of the date night will be even more amazing!

- ***One date night out of every month must be adventurous-*** it is ok to have dinner dates for the other three weeks, but at least once a month the date night has to be something "active" like going to an amusement park, zip-lining, going to an arcade or something of this nature. This keeps the youthful childlike aspect of the relationship alive in my opinion.

- ***Whenever possible, never visit the same place twice-*** In a city like Atlanta where a new restaurant opens every week, you and your partner should make it your duty to visit every single one of them. Different restaurants with different ambiance will bring different conversation and new insight into the person you are with.

Do Not Cry after the Fact!

When we first become Christians we are considered babies in Christ and treated as such. As our relationship with Christ grows we must grow and act as adults accepting responsibility for our actions and decisions. In adulthood there is an age of accountability where the excuse "I did not know" is no longer acceptable. The bible gives us a blue print to attain anything we want in life with God's help and instruction. When our human desires and emotions supersede God's best for our lives and we exercise free will, we must realize that as a responsible adult we and we alone are making this decision for our life. If our choice in a mate is a horrible decision, we cannot blame God for allowing us to make a free will decision as an adult. Be mindful that choosing a mate will probably be one of the most important decisions you will ever make. This decision will affect your finances, your degree of happiness, your health, and God's plan for your life. Since the mate we choose will affect our lives in so many areas, the choice should not be taken lightly.

The good news is that God can help us in our decision making process! God can show us where to find a suitable mate. When we meet someone God can show us who this person really is, good and bad qualities so that when we use our free will and choose a mate, we are fully aware of what we are getting ourselves into. Your relationship is the result of what you negotiated. When dating you must negotiate how you want to be treated, what you are willing to accept, and what you are not. When you say "I do" the contract is signed and God expects you to honor your commitment "Til death do you part". The bible refers to the Holy Spirit as a "helper" for a reason. So let's look to God to be our wingman and ensure that we are successful in finding, selecting, and marrying the spouse of our dreams!

Thank You for Reading

List of Must Haves:

1._____

2._____

3._____

4._____

5._____

6._____

7._____

Would like to have:

(Qualities that you would also like in a mate, but are not mandatory)

1._____

2._____

3._____

4._____

5._____

6._____

7._____

List of "Deal Breakers"

1._____

2._____

3._____

4._____

5._____

6._____

7._____

Scriptures

Proverbs 10:24

"The fear of the wicked will come upon him, And the desire of the righteous will be granted."

Matthew 7:16-17

"You will know them by their fruits. Do men gather grapes from thornbushes or figs from thistles? Even so, every good tree bears good fruit, but a bad tree bears bad fruit.

Proverbs 18:22

"He who finds a wife finds a good thing, and obtains favor from the lord."

James 1:7-8

"For let not that man suppose that he will receive anything from the Lord; he is a double-minded man, unstable in all his ways."

Habakkuk 2:2

"Write the vision And make it plain on tablets"

Jeremiah 1:5

"Before I formed you in the womb I knew you; Before you were born I sanctified you; I ordained you a prophet to the nations.

Matthew 7:9-11

"Or what man is there among you who, if his son asks for bread, will give him a stone? Or if he asks for a fish, will he give him a serpent? If you then, being evil, know how to give good gifts to your children, how much more will your father who is in heaven give good things to those who ask Him!"